Discovering Your Value

Joshua O. Okpara

Copyright © 2021 Joshua Okpara

All rights reserved.

ISBN:

DEDICATION

I Dedicate this book to you! Thank you for taking a bold step towards discovering just how valuable you are. My desire is that you take the secrets in this book and apply it in your life.

CONTENTS

	Introduction	I
1	How we define value	1
2	How value is determined	6
3	Signs that you are valuable (1)	10
4	Signs that you are valuable (2)	14
5	Takeaways	17
6	About the author	18

INTRODUCTION

Whether as a business owner, CEO, parent or a leader; this is one question that has crossed our minds at least once.

We all want to know our worth. Understanding it will help determine how we treat ourselves and how we allow others to treat us. But what is value? What determines if a person is valuable or not? Is it based on your experience, knowledge or the skill sets you have? Is value based on your material possession or is value based on reputation?

When your value is not understood, it can cause you to feel worthless, leading you to sell yourself and time for cheap. We all need to understand our value and know our worth in order to be effective, whether as a business owner, CEO, parent or leader.

In this book, I show you the secrets to determining your value and how to price your worth.

HOW WE DEFINE VALUE

It was 9:45pm on a Thursday night. Rain, strong winds and thunders were the only sounds that kept him up and alert as he awaited her text message. He was alone in his room, flickering the TV remote from channel to channel to keep his mind occupied, then it happened. Like the sound of an old school bell, his phone ringed. It was her. She sent him a message telling him of the conclusion of her thoughts on their relationship. It was over. She was done and wanted to see someone else.

Shocked, he dropped his phone and suddenly the sounds of the thunderstorm from the window became more silent until all he could hear was his rhythmic loud breathing. Then, it stopped.

Everything became dead silent as he began walking toward the kitchen to grab the butter knife.

Picking it up and putting it to his stomach, he began to cry, realizing that his worth was placed in their relationship and in her love for him. He thought they would stay together, but now her shocking display of disregard for their relationship created a need for him to end his life since he saw no need for it.

How could he possibly be worth anything when the one person that made him feel valuable no longer wants him? Right before he puts the knife in his stomach, the screen becomes black and a small line with the words "to be continued" came on the screen. The movie was over. Then it hit me. Although this was a scene from a movie, this showcased an area of my life that I never stopped to observe— where I placed my value.

I realized that just like the actor in the scene, I myself have placed my value on people or things that have failed to work out, which began to make me feel worthless. If the person or thing that I placed my value in decides to not need me anymore, that then determines my worth.

You see, we have a habit of determining value based on demand. "I am valuable because I am needed" or "I am valuable because I bring a certain solution to this problem." This leads to a toxic mindset because when who we are or the solution we bring is no longer in demand, we feel worthless. This is true for many business owners, CEOs, parents, and even leaders. "I am valuable because I am needed." When I stop being needed, I stop being valuable, and this couldn't be further from the truth.

Value is tied to purpose. I cannot understand my value if I don't know my purpose. Purpose is defined as the "reason for which something is done or created." That is another word that we are all striving to find alongside our value. What is my purpose? If I understand it, I can understand my value. If purpose is the reason for which something is created, this means that purpose is defined by the creator of the thing, not the created thing.

I have used Siri on my iPhone to find solutions to various problems, make phone calls, send text messages, and more. Siri seemed to know the answer to a lot of my question except one. "Hey Siri, why were you created?" After a long pause, the response was "I don't know what that means. If you like, I can search the web for 'Hey Siri, why were you created?' "I was shocked.

As sophisticated a technology as Siri was, this virtual assistant couldn't answer the question to why it was created; yet, in answering my question, it was fulfilling purpose. What's created cannot explain why it was created unless informed by the creator.

The creator determines the purpose of the created. A burger cannot speak for itself as to why it was formed, but the cook can explain the need that burger was made to meet because the cook created it. A car cannot speak for itself as to why it was created, but the manufacturer can ascribe its purpose to the user. Why is that important? Not only does the creator of a thing determine its purpose. The creator also determines its value. The creator of a thing determines the value of the thing based on its purpose!

This begs the question: who created us? We can be certain it was not our parents. Although they birthed us, surely, we as humans must've been created. After vast research, I found that the only solution to this problem is found in going to the very beginning of creation. Human species have been found dating back over 2 million years ago. Who was the first human and who created that human? Better yet, what was the purpose for the creation of that human?

We see a clue in the Bible. In the book of Genesis chapter 1, we get a small insight to the beginning of creation. The beginning of the chapter says, "In the beginning, God created the Heaven and the Earth." It then goes into details of how that happened in the next verses.

What stood out to me was the creation of man in Genesis 1:26-27, which says, "And God said, let us make man in our image, after our likeness: and let them have dominion over the fish of the sea, and over the fowl of the air, and over the cattle, and over all the earth, and over every creeping thing that creepeth upon the earth. So, God created man in His own image, in the image of God created He him; male and female created He them."

In these verses, we are exposed to the creation and purpose of humans. We were created by God and purposed to dominate the earth. If, therefore, God created us and purposed us to dominate, as created beings, we cannot determine our value. The value of a person or a thing can only be determined by the creator of the person or thing, which begs the question: how does God value us?

HOW VALUE IS DETERMINED

I still remember the day like it was yesterday. I needed a car, and it has always been my dream to buy a Tesla. I woke up that morning determined to get one with the $500 in my bank account. I was excited as I walked into the store and was given the opportunity of a lifetime to test drive the car. We drove around the block and immediately I was sold.

Everything from the self-driving capabilities to the app features in the car made me a believer. I knew I had to get this car and I needed to today, so I popped the big question: "how much is it?" The answer I was given was enough to send me home disappointed.

I was a college student with little in my bank account and a big love for the car. My love for the car made me see it as something so valuable, I was willing to give my only $500 as a down payment just to get it.

Unfortunately, my value for the car doesn't determine the true value of the car. Although I loved and cherish the car, I did not manufacture it; therefore, I could not determine its worth and value. The manufacturer determines the value, and I either had to afford the worth of the car or wait until I could afford it.

My demand for the car doesn't change the worth or value of it. It was not the value or price that had to change. My expectations had to be brought up to match that of the manufacturer. The manufacturer understands the work and expense put into the car, leading it up to that price point. The investment of designing and creating the car created the value they placed on it. This is a principle that many manufacturers, such as Lamborghini, Ferrari, and Rolls Royce, follow. The worth of the car is not determined by the purchaser but determined by the creator.

Whether I thought a Lamborghini was worth $50 or $50,000, it wouldn't change the price of the car. I simply just wouldn't be their needed customer. They don't spend time trying to convince me on the worth of the car. They simply await the right customer. When you understand your worth and value, you don't spend time trying to convince others who don't see it.

In Genesis 1:26, we see the intention of God in creating humans. With that purpose in mind came the value. God didn't stop at stating His intention for us to dominate. After creating humans, He went ahead to give value to His creation and declaring its worth before anything or anyone declared it. In Genesis 1:31, it states, "And God saw everything that He had made, and behold, it was very good."

The Bible was explicit in exclaiming God's thought on His creation. Being the creator, He placed the value of being "very good" on us, declaring our worth not just to us, but to the heavens and earth. Therefore, it is that value that we are to internalize and uphold.

We, as created beings, have not been given the authority to determine our value. We didn't create ourselves. Value can only be determined or proclaimed by the creator of a thing. It is the value that the creator placed on the created that stands. A Tesla car cannot determine its value. Neither can I, the consumer, determine its worth. The manufacturer determines the value and we either adhere to it or we simply are not the right consumers.

This is critical because if value is placed in the hands of the consumer, then the value will be determined by demand and affordability.

If I had excess funds to spend, my desire for a new car would be less compared to someone who had no money. The value I would place on the car would be different than that of another person who may not be able to afford it. Therefore, we must be careful not to value ourselves based on others value of us.

Whether someone sees you as valuable or worthless, their opinions are irrelevant because they cannot determine your worth. They didn't create you. Only your creator can determine your worth and this creator has called you 'very good', which means that is the standard others must adhere to. If they don't see the value that the creator placed on you, they are simply not worthy of your essence

SIGNS THAT YOU ARE VALUABLE (PART 1)

If you've ever been to the water isle at any grocery store, then, like me, you'll be shocked to see the varieties available with different prices. What makes one bottle of water more or less expensive than the next? Brand.

Today, value is now based on brand more than it is on quality. The big-name brand will sell at a higher price point than that of an unknown brand. I remember when I used to work in the tech department of a grocery store selling headphones. Customers were always looking for the name brand that everyone was wearing or the brand that their favorite celebrity uses.

Companies understand this and market their products using celebrities that will push the value of the product. An unknown product could have essentially the same quality as the well-known brand but will sell less because of its brand. People value things based on its brand.

The brand determines the value. To brand a product is to put your label on the product. Essentially, you are creating an extension of yourself, and when consumers see it, they see you.

Companies spend more now on marketing than they ever have before, ensuring that their brand awareness is great so consumers will be inclined to purchase it. This tactic did not just start today. It has been a strategy from the very beginning of creation.

God used this very strategy in creating man. It was the brand that He gave man that caused Him to declare man's value as very good. In Genesis 2:7, we see the strategy God uses in creating humans. It says, "And the LORD God formed man of the dust of the ground and breathed into his nostrils the breath of life; and man became a living soul." The word 'breathes' in the original language the Bible was written in is translated as "Spirit".

God formed us, then breathed His Spirit into Human, giving us the ability to be a Soul. Some may ask, "Why was this strategy used?" Remember; it was God's intent in Genesis 1:26 for us to be created in His image and likeness, and to dominate. For us to achieve our purpose, He formed us and breathed His Spirit into us. His Spirit in us then became His method of branding us, which led to the value of us being "very good."

From the beginning of creation, you have been branded. Given a purpose and given value. God branded you with His Spirit. Gave you the purpose to dominate through that Spirit and placed the value of you being "very good." He goes through this extensive process to expose us to the truth that we cannot brand or place value on ourselves. We have been given the mandate to uphold that value placed on us.

A product cannot determine its brand, purpose or value. The creator of the product determines that. Likewise, we cannot determine our brand, purpose or value. We did not create ourselves; we can only live up to the value placed on us.

However, there are times when we may not feel valuable. These are times when we lose sight of purpose and forget that we have been branded. At times, this is a result of listening to the competition.

In business, companies fighting to be the most consumed by the customer will attempt to bash the other company's product to praise their own. This is common in every industry. Every company desire to be the best in their industry and with this desire comes competition. This competition for the top of the market at times causes companies to spend millions in marketing to advertise why their product is a better option than the competition.

No company will praise the competing product. At times, they will bash it as being ineffective compared to their own. Their goal is to get the consumer to find their product more valuable than their competitor; and they will spend millions trying to achieve this goal.

Sometimes, the company with the best quality gets the most competition coming against it. They face the biggest opposition and the most campaigns designed to devalue their product. A company that knows it's worth understands that, because of its value in the market, it will face opposition. But they don't see the opposition as an issue. The more companies that revolt against them, the more confident they are about their product because the opposition, to sabotage them, shows how valuable they are.

The success or failure of the opposition doesn't change the value of the company because, again, the opposition does not determine the value of a product they did not create. Nonetheless, opposition is a great indication of how valuable a product is; yet, we oftentimes run away from opposition, forgetting the truth that opposition is a sign of value.

SIGNS THAT YOU ARE VALUABLE (PART 2)

As a created being, one major sign that you're valuable is the opposition you face.

As this works in the natural, so it works in the spiritual. God, who is our creator, has a competitor who seeks to steal, kill and destroy everything that God creates.

This competitor understands that he cannot devalue us because he didn't create us; yet he strategically plans to change the way we see ourselves and it is critical to understand that it is because he understands how valuable we are. Therefore, he desperately wants us to not see that value.

This enemy of God strategically plants thoughts

in the mind of humans, causing them to think they're not valuable. He plants thoughts like, "You're not good enough. God doesn't like you. No one likes you. You're not worthy. You're a bad father. You're a bad mother. You're a bad sister. You're a bad brother. You're a bad leader. You're a bad employee. You're a bad employer."

Although these implanted thoughts don't change your value, the goal is to get you to lose sight of it. If I can get you to think that you're worthless, it will change how you treat yourself and how you allow others to treat you. This strategy unfortunately has been working for centuries and it has caused many to fall into depression, anxiety, thoughts of suicide, and other mental health issues because they lost sight of their worth.

Do you know that opposition is a sign that you're valuable? The enemy strives hard to attack God's creation through various means, all to cause them to lose sight of their value. He will bring bad marriages, a bad upbringing, the loss of a job, friends, family members or a relationship, pain, loneliness, abuse, lack, and anything possible to get you to lose sight of your worth.

These things are a sign that you're worthy. They cannot define your value because they didn't create you. Your value has already been determined from the very beginning. You were formed, purposed to dominate, and branded with the Spirit of God. There's no other brand greater or better than the Spirit of God.

DISCOVERING YOUR VALUE

Do you know that you're valuable? Do you understand your worth is not based on anyone's opinion of you, nor your opinion of yourself? Value cannot be determined by the created, only the creator, and your creator valued you as being "very good." The question is not whether you're valuable, but whether you see yourself the way your creator sees you.

TAKEAWAYS

1. You are a created being, created by a creator.
2. The creator determines the purpose of the created.
3. Your purpose has been pre-determined by the creator.
4. Your purpose determines your Value.
5. Your brand gives you value.
6. You have been branded by your creator. He branded you with His Spirit.
7. Your creator valued you as being "very good."
8. Opposition is a sign that you're valuable. Embrace it.
9. You cannot change your value. Because it has already been pre-determined, you simply must live up to it.
10. We must therefore treat ourselves as valuable and require others around us to do the same.

ABOUT THE AUTHOR

Joshua Okpara is an entrepreneur, Best-Selling Author, Motivational Speaker, Pastor, Husband, Father and Artist.

He is a strategy and business coach who specializes in helping clients find their passion and generate income from it.

He is also the founder of the prestigious organization, The Dedicated Men, that focuses on creating a brotherhood of financially literate leaders, entrepreneurs, scholars and professionals, who know their identity in Christ.

He has written 5 best-selling books such as *How To Deal With Real Pain In Real Time, 31 Days To A Better You, She's the one, but you're not the one yet, and The Gift Of Singleness*; sold nationally and internationally.

Joshua is known for his charisma, leadership, and his passion for Music. He is married to Charmecia Okpara and together they raise their son Josiah King Okpara. He is currently the Founder/Pastor of The Faith Filled Church, located in Lewisville Tx.

ABOUT THE AUTHOR

CONNECT WITH ME

Facebook: @joshuaokparalive

Twitter: @joshua_o_okpara

Instagram: @joshua_o_okpara

LinkedIn: http://linkedin.com/in/joshuaokpara

Email: info@joshuaokpara.com

Website: https://Joshuaokpara.com

Made in the USA
Middletown, DE
24 August 2023